D0269439

Arts and Crafts of ANCIENT EGYPT

Ting Morris

Illustrated by Emma Young

An Appleseed Editions book

First published in 2006 by Franklin Watts
338 Euston Road, London NW1 3BH

Franklin Watts Australia
Hachette Children's Books
Level 17/207 Kent St, Sydney, NSW 2000

Created by Appleseed Editions Ltd, Well House,
Friars Hill, Guestling, East Sussex TN35 4ET

Artwork by Emma Young
Designed by Helen James
Edited by Mary-Jane Wilkins
Picture research by Su Alexander

ISBN 0 7496 6741 9

Dewey Classification: 704.03'931

A CIP catalogue for this book is available from the British Library

Photograph acknowledgements
Front cover Roger Wood/Corbis; page 5t Sandro Vannini/Corbis, b Gianni Dagli Orti/Corbis; 7t Ruggero Vanni/Corbis, b Araldo De Luca/Corbis; 8 Gianni Dagli Orti/Corbis; 9 Archivo Iconografico, S.A./Corbis; 10 Roger Wood/Corbis; 12 Brooklyn Museum of Art/Corbis; 13 copyright the Trustees of The British Museum; 14 Erich Lessing/AKG Images; 15, 16 & 18 copyright the Trustees of The British Museum; 19 Roger Wood/Corbis; 20 & 21 copyright the Trustees of The British Museum; 22 O.Alamany & E.Vicens/Corbis; 24 Werner Forman/Corbis; 25t copyright the Trustees of The British Museum, b Archivo Iconografico, S.A./Corbis; 26 Brooklyn Museum of Art/Corbis; 27t Sandro Vannini/Corbis, b Gianni Dagli Orti/Corbis; 28 Erich Lessing/AKG Images

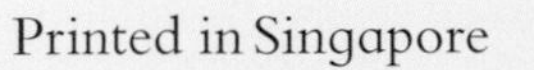
Printed in Singapore

Contents

The world of the ancient Egyptians

More than 7000 years ago, groups of people settled in a fertile region beside the River Nile in north-east Africa. They grew wheat and barley and kept herds of goats and sheep, and they eventually formed two kingdoms. Lower Egypt covered the marshy land of the Nile delta, near the Mediterranean Sea. Upper Egypt was further south. Around 3150 BC the two lands became a single kingdom which flourished for almost 3000 years.

The ancient Egyptians built huge monuments, including tombs for their kings and temples for their gods. They decorated some buildings with paintings and sculptures, and modern archaeologists have discovered many examples of the Egyptians' skill as artists and craftworkers.

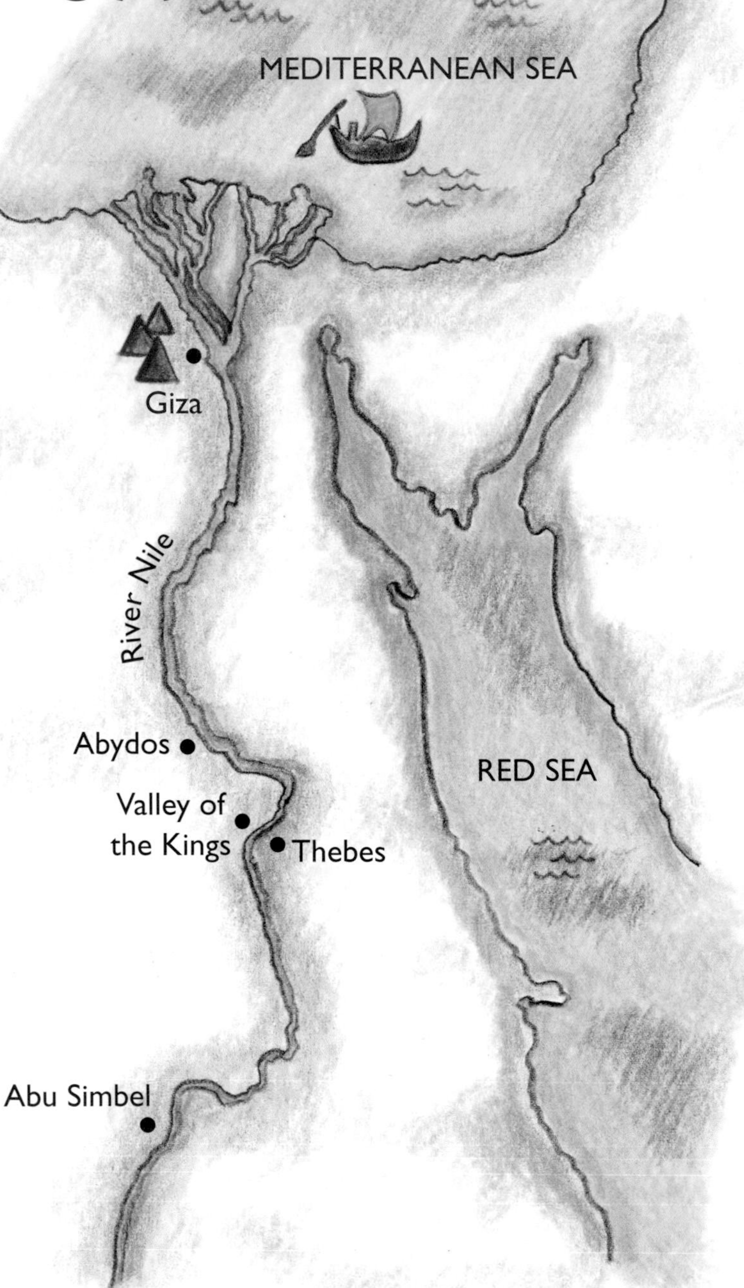

The ancient Egyptians based their lives around the River Nile. They lived on what they called the black land – fertile soil produced by the rich, dark mud spread by the river's annual flood.

This slab is the Narmer Palette. It shows the first king (top left) wearing the crown of Lower Egypt, marching towards rows of beheaded enemies. Beneath are two lionesses with long necks. At the bottom the king is shown as a raging bull.

Early kings

A king named Narmer was the first to rule united Egypt. He was the founder of the First Dynasty, and his people linked him with their falcon god Horus, the main god of kingship. Some of the earliest surviving Egyptian art comes from this period, including some shield-shaped slabs made of slate. They are called palettes, and many had carvings of wild animals. Ancient Egyptians may have used them in magic ceremonies to make their hunters successful.

High Priest of Ptah

The ancient Egyptians believed that a god named Ptah invented the arts. Ptah became the special god of all artists and craftworkers. Because of this, the god's human High Priest was known as the supreme leader of craftsmen, and he was in charge of all Egyptian works of art. Artists often showed Ptah as a mummy with a shaven head and a tight-fitting cap.

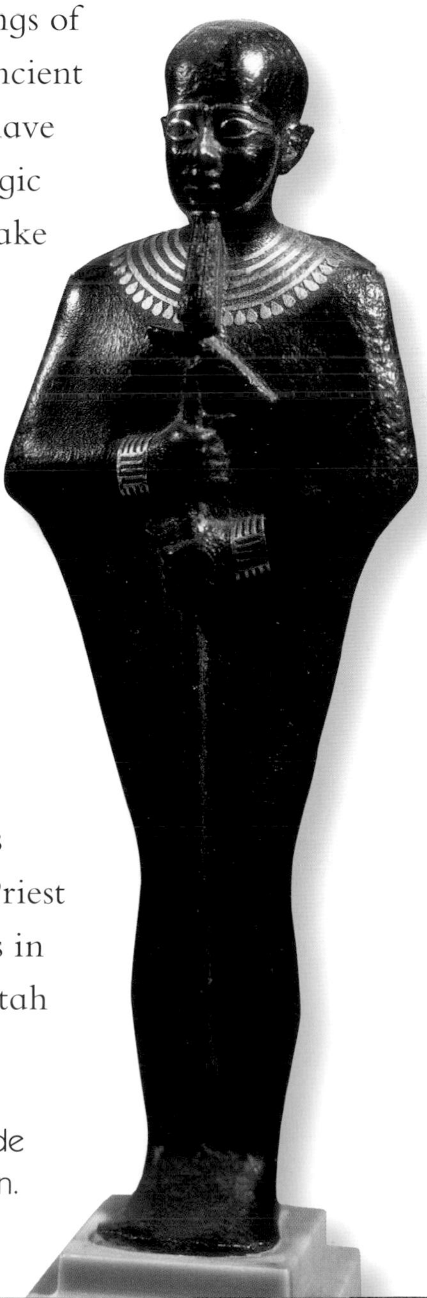

This bronze statuette of Ptah was made in ancient Egypt by a master craftsman.

Statues and sculptors

Sculptors produced their art in workshops set up by the king, priests or other important people, as did other groups of artists and craftsmen. In each workshop a master craftsman worked with a group of assistants and apprentices on a single large piece of sculpture.

To start a statue, a designer drew a grid on the sides of a block of stone. He then added outlines of the shape to be carved from the block. Many carvings were then coated with a glue-like substance and painted in bright colours. The master craftsman oversaw the whole process and carved important figures or parts of scenes himself.

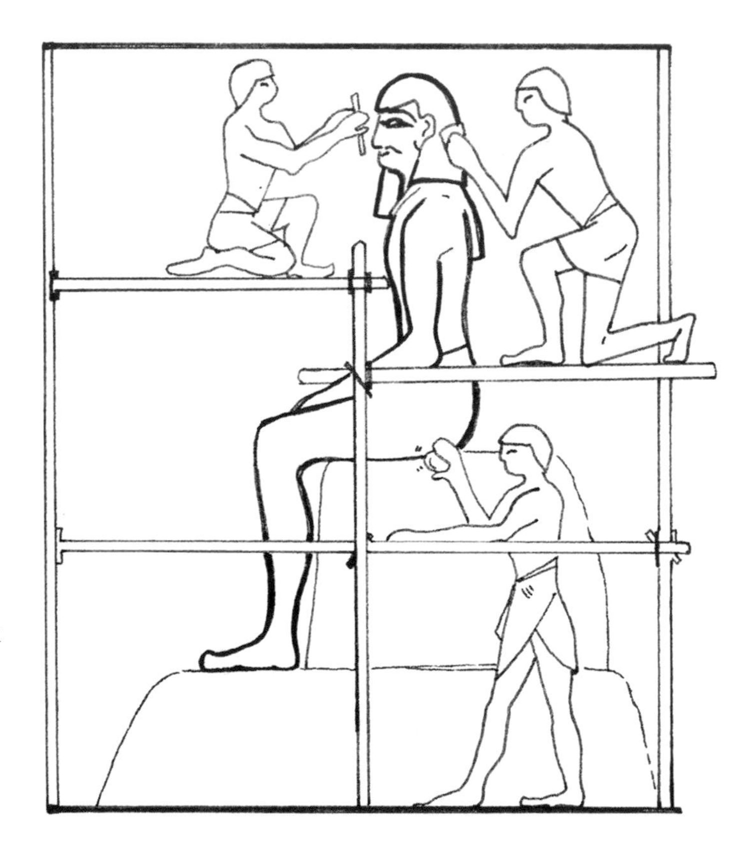

This drawing of part of a wall painting shows a group of sculptors working together to carve a statue. Each sculptor is working on a different part of the huge statue. The wall painting this drawing is based on was found in the tomb of an important official, who died around 1430 BC.

Painted reliefs

Egyptian sculptors did much of their work in relief. This means that they carved figures or designs so they stood out from a background of stone. They specialized in two types: raised relief figures which stood out from the background surface, and sunk relief figures carved into the background. Artists often painted the reliefs in brilliant colours, but most of the paint has worn away from these. Many reliefs were made during the period historians call the Old Kingdom (roughly 2700–2200 BC).

You can still see some paint on this raised relief, from the tomb of a pharaoh's daughter named Idut, who died around 2330 BC. The cattle were offerings to help her in the afterlife.

In the service of the king

During the period of the Middle Kingdom (about 2050–1650 BC), some of the best artists and sculptors worked in the service of the king. They portrayed him in various ways and often gave him the body of a lion. This is the figure we call a sphinx, which the Egyptians saw as a guardian of sacred places, such as the king's tomb. Sculptors carved the figures using hard stone hammers with wooden handles, as well as copper and bronze tools. They smoothed the carved surface with rubbing stones and a sandy paste.

This sphinx shows the head of Ahmose II, who wears a striped head-cloth known as a nemes. Only a few sculptures of this popular ruler have survived.

Paint and painters

The oldest Egyptian wall paintings were found in a tomb that is more than 5000 years old. They show people and animals. Like sculptors, Egyptian painters worked in teams, decorating tombs, temples and palaces under the guidance of a master craftsman. None of them signed their pictures. The writing you see on paintings gives the names of the people shown in them, or a description of the action.

Painters usually arranged the figures in their pictures in rows. They were portrayed in formal poses and had perfect features. Paintings always show one eye, the shoulders and the chest of the human body from the front, with the face, legs and arms turned to the side. Ancient Egyptian painters worked on rock walls in temples. They usually painted on plastered walls, which had to be prepared.

This wall painting is in the tomb of the young king Tutankhamun, who died in 1327 BC. It shows him between Anubis, the jackal-headed god of the dead, and the sky-goddess Hathor.

This picture, painted around 1350 BC, shows the scribe Nebamun with his wife and daughter, hunting for birds in the Nile marshes.

Preparing a wall

First the painters coated a wall with straw and mud, then they covered it with a layer of plaster. They divided the dry surface into a grid of squares using string dipped in ink and stretched out into horizontal and vertical lines. An outline draughtsman then drew on it.

After the painters had coloured in the picture, the draughtsman restored the outlines, usually in dark red-brown or black. Finally, a scribe wrote the inscription in hieroglyphs – like a picture caption in this book.

Creating colours

Paint was made from natural substances, ground into powder and mixed with water and a binder (such as vegetable gum). This made the paint stick. Yellow, red and brown colours came from a mineral called ochre. Blue was made by heating mixed sand, copper and natron. White came from lime, and black from soot or manganese. Artists put on the paint in flat blocks of colour with no shading.

Paint a temple wall

The ancient Egyptians dedicated their temples to the most important gods and goddesses, as well as to kings and queens. They kept a golden statue of an individual god in an inner sanctuary. Priests looked after it, and ordinary Egyptians were not allowed in to worship. They only saw the golden statues when they were carried out on festival days. Temples were decorated inside and out with reliefs and paintings.

This painted wall relief is inside the Temple of Rameses II at Abydos, where the Egyptians worshipped Osiris, the god of death and rebirth. It shows three images of Horus, the falcon-headed son of Osiris, who was the king's protector.

Paint your own temple wall

You will need: a large piece of cardboard • plaster of Paris or primer • white ready-mixed paint • paintbrushes • a ruler • charcoal or a soft-lead pencil • brown, blue, red, yellow, green and black poster paints.

1 Cut a 50 x 40cm piece from a large cardboard box. Mix plaster of Paris powder with water until it is as thick as paint and brush the paste over the wall. Or use a primer for the undercoat. When it is dry, paint it with a layer of ready-mixed white paint and leave it to dry again.

2 Use a ruler and soft pencil to draw grid lines 5cm apart. Draw nine horizontal and seven vertical lines, to make 5cm squares across the wall. Draw the outline of Horus on the grid as shown here, using the squares as a guide. This way you can make the picture five times bigger.

3 Colour Horus. Copy the details and colours in the finished picture. Leave the paint to dry.

4 Mix white paint with a splash of blue and black for a light grey background. Apply this evenly round Horus and paint out the squares. Wait for the paint to dry before outlining Horus. Use a fine brush and black paint mixed with brown.

5 Write a caption in hieroglyphs. Copy the ones in the picture or make up your own.

The ancient Egyptians thought Horus brought protection, so you could keep your wall painting in your room for good luck.

In the potter's workshop

Mud from the River Nile made Egypt fertile. The Egyptians used the mud as a source of clay for making pots. When the pots were fired in a kiln, they turned a red-brown colour. From the earliest times potters made all sorts of containers from clay. They shaped the clay to make storage jars, cooking pots and serving vessels.

More than 5000 years ago, craftsmen were using ochre paint to decorate pots with images of people and animals. Archaeologists have pieced together many pots from fragments called potsherds. These tell us about everyday life in ancient Egypt.

This bowl was made from Nile clay about 3400 BC. It is decorated with boat designs that show life on the river. The Egyptians may have placed the bowl above a tomb so they could make liquid offerings to the dead.

This blue faience bowl shows a pool with lotus flowers. The pool was a symbol of rebirth, and bowls like this were placed in tombs to be useful in the afterlife.

Using the wheel

After about 2700 BC, or even earlier, potters began using a wheel to turn the clay. This made it easier to shape pots. The simple wheel was a mud and straw turntable attached to a polished stone set into a smooth stone base. The potter spun the wheel with one hand and shaped his pot with the other. Around 500 BC, a potter invented a foot-operated wheel which allowed craftsmen to use both hands to shape the clay.

Brilliant material

As well as clay, the Egyptians used a material they called *tjehenet*, meaning brilliant. We call it faience. It was made from crushed desert sand mixed with lime, ash or natron. Potters added water and then shaped objects by hand or using clay moulds. They glazed the objects to make them shiny. The Egyptians used faience tiles to decorate pyramid tombs, as well as in jewellery. Faience looked like gemstones such as turquoise.

Precious metals and gemstones

The ancient Egyptians found a wealth of minerals and metals in the desert surrounding their land. The first metal they used was copper, which they mined in the desert to the east of the Nile 5000 years ago. Copper was useful for tools, and was also made into small statues.

By 2000 BC the ancient Egyptians were adding tin to copper to make bronze, which was a harder metal. They melted the metals over charcoal fires and poured them into clay moulds. To make their fires hotter they blew air through bellows. Later, when the metal had cooled, the metalworker shaped it with a hammer. A similar method was used for silver, which was known as the white metal. The early Egyptians valued it more highly than gold.

This fine bronze statuette of the cat-goddess Bastet is 27cm high.

Beautiful jewellery

From very early times the Egyptians turned precious metals and brilliant gemstones into rings, bracelets, pendants and other jewellery. Wonderful jewellery was found in the tomb of Tutankhamun. The Egyptians thought the blue stone called lapis lazuli imitated the blue of the heavens, and they imported as much as they could from Badakhshan (in modern Afghanistan). They mined blue-green turquoise in the eastern desert, and jewellers also used purple amethyst.

This pendant was made around 1890 BC in the form of a winged scarab beetle. It has a frame of electrum (a natural mixture of gold and silver) and is inlaid with blue lapis lazuli, red carnelian and green feldspar.

The divine metal

The Egyptians thought that gold was a divine metal, perhaps because it never loses its shiny colour and looks like the sun. They believed that gold was the flesh of the sun god Ra and other deities, while their bones were made of silver.

The Egyptians dug gold mines throughout the eastern desert and the south of Egypt, and sent soldiers to protect the explorers who looked for new goldfields. Very important people had death masks and other funeral objects made of gold. Egyptian goldsmiths were never short of work, and their raw material was described around 1350 BC as being as plentiful as dirt.

Make an amulet

Egyptian amulets were a kind of good-luck charm. The Egyptians believed that these small ornaments protected the wearer against evil, danger and illness. Jewellers made them in the shape of animals, plants and sacred objects. Amulets were often placed with mummies to protect the dead on their journey to the next world. Some were in the shape of symbols, such as the knot of Isis, the goddess who was the symbolic mother of the Egyptian king.

The knot of Isis amulet is made of red jasper and was put around the neck of the dead to give them the protection of the goddess Isis. Other amulets were made in the shape of body parts.

Make your own knot of Isis

You will need: air-hardening clay • a modelling tool • a toothpick • a rolling pin • red and green poster paints • varnish • a foil-covered board • a ribbon.

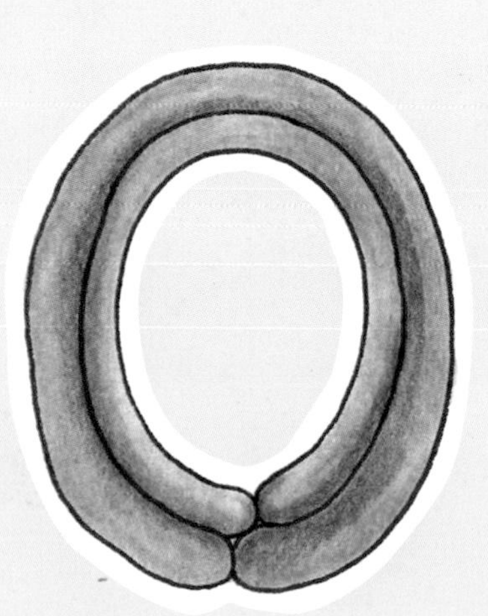

1 Knead a lump of clay until it is soft. Roll two pieces back and forth on a foil-covered board to make sausage-shaped tubes. Make one a little longer than the other. Flatten them, moisten the edges and stick them together.

2 Roll a thin strip of clay and mark out four holes with a toothpick. Fix the strip on top of the coils.

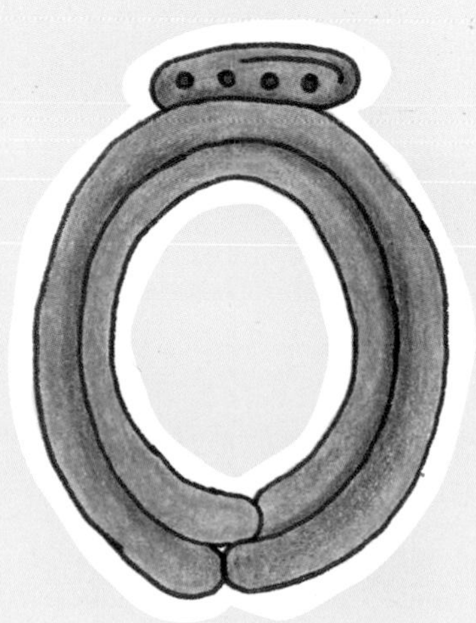

3 Flatten a ball of clay with your hand until it is as thick as the coils, or roll it out with a rolling pin. Use a modelling tool to cut out the shape and mark it.

4 Moisten the bottom edge of the loop and the top of the main shape, and stick them together. Smooth and flatten the joint with your finger. Then draw in the detail with a toothpick.

5 When the amulet is dry, paint it red. Allow the paint to dry before varnishing it. Tie a ribbon through the loop and wear it as a pendant so its magical powers protect you.

Use the same method to make a hand. Roll out five finger-thick tubes and shape them into a hand. Pierce a hole in the middle of the wrist with a toothpick, so you can wear it as a pendant. When the hand is dry, paint and varnish it.

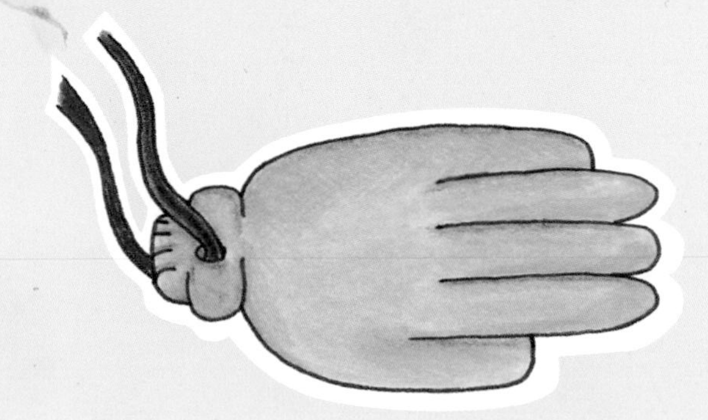

Baskets and matting

The ancient Egyptians found all the materials they needed for making baskets and mats on the banks of the Nile. They made rope from tall, strong halfa grass, which they twisted into cords and used for twining. They used the rind of papyrus stems (a reed that grew beside the Nile) in the same way, and plaited cords to make mats. The Egyptians used these on the floors and roofs of their mud-brick houses.

The ancient Egyptians made baskets from the leaves of the doum palm, and later from date-palm leaves. Sometimes they used rushes and sedges from the Nile marshes. The earliest Egyptian coffins were simple baskets, and later baskets ranged from small bags for carrying food and other goods to large storage containers for clothes.

This small lidded basket was made of doum-palm fibre around 1400 BC. It was probably placed in a tomb so its contents would go with the dead person into the afterlife.

Techniques of basketwork

From the earliest times most baskets were made by coiling. Basket-makers started by tightly wrapping bundles of fibres to form coils, which they stitched together. They made the sides of the basket by winding and binding coils upwards from the base. Other baskets were twined, by weaving strands over a framework of spokes. When the basket was finished, the spokes could not be seen. If a basket was plaited, the spokes and strands were woven together, giving an attractive result that was less sturdy. Basket-makers sometimes used coloured stitching or plaiting to make geometric designs.

Heavy work

People used baskets for carrying bread, vegetables, meat and other household items. Women usually carried the loads, holding the baskets on their heads with one hand, as they still do in parts of Egypt today. Scientists studying ancient skeletons have found that many women damaged their necks by supporting heavy loads on their head.

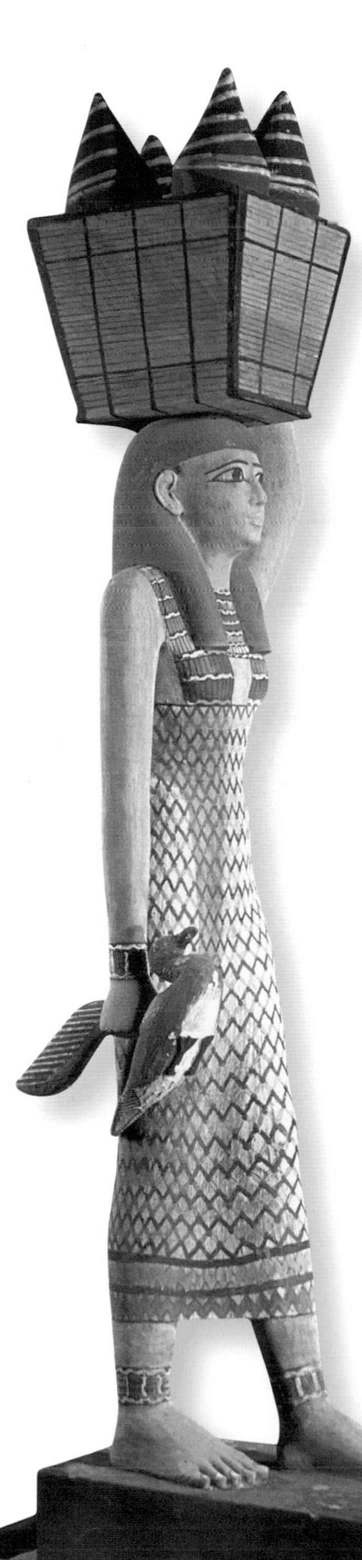

This painted wooden statuette shows a young woman carrying a basket of food. She gracefully balances the basket with one hand while holding a live duck in the other. The food was an offering, and the statuette was found in a tomb dating from just after 2000 BC.

Woodwork and furniture

Egyptian woodworkers used palm wood and wood from acacia, sycamore, fig and tamarisk trees. But the best wood was cedar from Lebanon. Carpenters cut planks by pulling a long saw through the timber. They used tools with copper blades to make furniture, boats, coffins, statues, musical instruments, board games and toys.

Tables and stools

Ordinary Egyptians probably had little furniture. Some may have had wooden beds, with a rush mattress and a wooden headrest instead of a pillow.

They stored linen and other household items in wooden boxes. They also had low tables and stools, which were quite simple, though by 1800 BC carpenters were making folding stools. They seem to have specialized in designing and making light furniture that was useful for travelling merchants and soldiers.

The low scooped stool (left) was more common than the backed chair (right) owned by wealthy people. Someone important must have owned this chair, which has feet in the shape of lion's paws.

Painted wood

Before they painted wood the ancient Egyptians covered it with a thin layer of mixed plaster and glue, which acted as a background and gave a smooth finish. Sculptors used chisels and other tools to carve wooden statues and models which are more lifelike than ones carved from stone. Craftsmen also made and painted wooden mummy cases and *shabtis* (small figurines put in tombs to help the dead person in the afterlife). As well as painting wood, craftworkers also used inlays of ivory and gold.

Canopic jars were used as containers for a dead person's internal organs, and were placed in tombs with the mummy. The lids of these painted wooden jars show the four sons of Horus – baboon-headed Hapy, jackal-headed Duamutef, falcon-headed Qebhsenuef and human-headed Imsety.

Make a mummy case

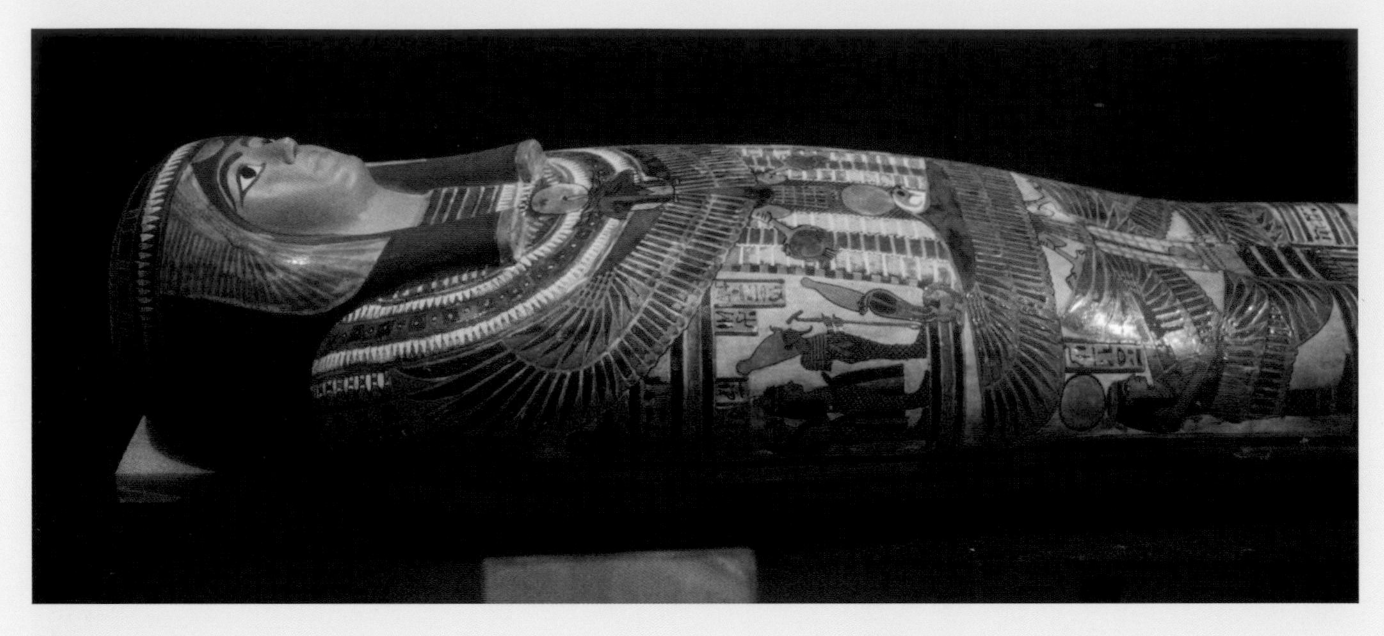

The Egyptians believed that a dead person's body should be preserved as a mummy so it could live on after death. The mummy was put into a coffin or mummy case made of wood or cartonnage (a material made of layers of linen or papyrus glued together). Royal mummies were often put inside two or three cases which all fitted into each other. The Egyptians decorated the cases with pictures of gods and magic spells both inside and outside.

This is the cartonnage mummy case of a woman named Shepenkhonsu, who was called 'the mistress of the house'. She died around 1000 BC.

Make your own mummy case

You will need: a long balloon • wallpaper paste (fungicide-free) • PVA glue • a craft knife • string • a pair of scissors • white ready-mixed paint • gold paint • black, red, blue, yellow and green poster paints • paintbrushes • newspaper • sequins.

1 Blow up the balloon to about 35cm in length and tie the end. Wind some string around the balloon to make a head and body shape. Tear newspaper into thin strips about 2cm wide.

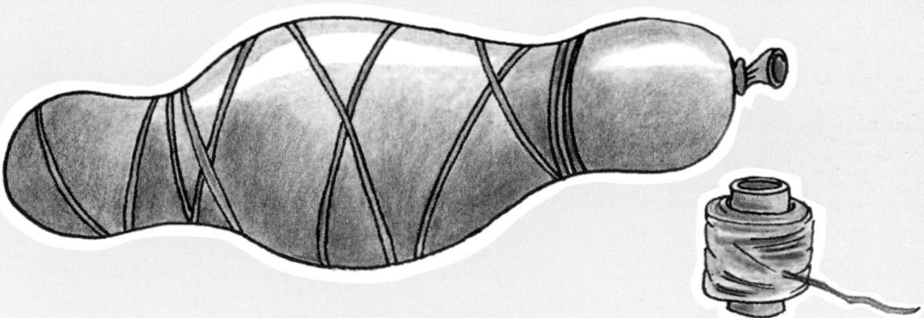

2 Mix the wallpaper paste and coat the strips with it. Pull each strip between your finger and thumb to remove any lumps. Cover the balloon with a layer of paper, making sure you keep the mummy shape. Build up four layers, then leave the paper to dry.

3 Add another four layers of coated newspaper strips. Make the last layer especially smooth. Leave it in a warm place to dry overnight.

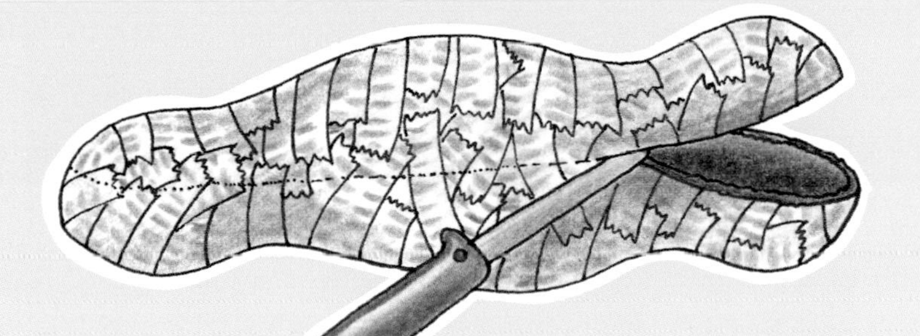

4 Draw a line around the papier-mâché balloon and with adult help cut along the line with a craft knife, using a sawing action. Peel away the balloon. Trim the cut edges with scissors to make an even rim. Dilute a little PVA glue with water to a thin cream and use it to cover the edges with small pieces of newspaper. Leave it to dry.

5 Paint both halves white, inside and out. When the paint is dry, paint the inside gold. Leave it to dry. Paint the mummy's face and collar, then paint a pattern and hieroglyphs down the front.

6 Decorate the body. Paint the lower half of the mummy case with green, blue and red patterns. Put a thin line of glue all around the edge of the bottom half and stick on sequins and then varnish it. Leave it to dry.

Use this beautiful mummy case to store your precious things.

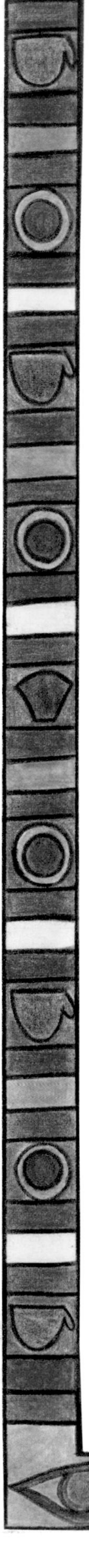

Timeless beauty

The ancient Egyptians cared a great deal about their appearance, but their clothes were practical too. They were mostly made of white linen, which was light and airy. Working men wore short kilts, while women usually wore long dresses.

The linen came from flax plants planted and harvested by the men. Women spun the plant fibres into thread before weaving this into pieces of linen on a simple flat loom. Some women did their own weaving at home, but large quantities of linen were made in workshops.

This wooden model, made around 1900 BC, shows boatmen wearing the simple linen kilt of the time.

Classy dress

High-ranking women wore the finest linen, and in later times pleated dresses came into fashion. The linen was sometimes dyed in colourful patterns, and women also wore bead netting over tight-fitting dresses. Hairstyles were another way of showing a person's importance, and wealthy women had their own hairdressers. Long, layered wigs were fashionable, usually made from human hair, or sometimes plant fibres.

This tomb painting shows Ahmose-Nefertari, the wife of King Ahmose I (who reigned 1550–1525 BC). She is wearing a flowing pleated dress and an elaborate headdress.

Made-up faces

Both men and women wore make-up. The Egyptians made cosmetics from minerals ground up and mixed with water to form a paste. They made black eye-powder, or kohl, from galena, red lipstick from iron oxide and pink powder from ochre. The Egyptians coloured their hair with henna, just as people do today. They used oils and fats to make cosmetic creams and perfumes.

In this banquet scene the female guests wear fine white and yellow dresses. They have heavy wigs, with incense cones made of scented oils on top. The cones melted in the heat to perfume the wigs.

Words and pictures

The Egyptians were using their own writing system by about 3250 BC. We call this script hieroglyphics, from the Greek for sacred carving, but the Egyptians used the same word (sekh) for writing, drawing and painting. Writing was an art in itself, as many hieroglyphic signs were simple diagrams – such as a circle for the sun, or a small figure of a seated man for man.

The Egyptians used hieroglyphics for sacred inscriptions in temples and tombs, as well as on stone slabs honouring important people. Very few people could write or read. Scribes wrote on papyrus, a material made from reeds that grew beside the Nile. Our word paper comes from the name of this plant.

The Book of the Dead

The papyrus scrolls we call the Book of the Dead were known to ancient Egyptians as the spell for coming forth by day. The beautifully painted scrolls contained spells supposed to overcome the dangers of the underworld. They were placed in coffins and sometimes inside mummy bandaging, to protect the dead person on the difficult journey through the underworld to the afterlife.

This carved limestone slab, called a stela, honours a person named Anhorkhawi. At the top is a picture of Re-Horakhty, a sun-god shown as a hawk. The stela was carved about 1160 BC, during the reign of Rameses III.

This papyrus Book of the Dead was found in the tomb of a man called Maiherpri, who died about 1450 BC. He was called a 'fan-bearer on the right hand of the king'. Maiherpri is shown greeting cows, which stand before offerings of food.

Scribes

The job of scribe was very important in ancient Egypt. Scribes learned hundreds of hieroglyphs, and they had to be able to write them clearly. They wrote on papyrus, with a pen made from a reed, which was brushed over a cake of pigment. They wrote mainly in black made from soot, and used ochre red for headings and to highlight dates. Only a very small number of boys (and no girls) went to school to learn hieroglyphics and possibly become a scribe.

This sculpture shows a royal scribe in the traditional pose. He sits cross-legged, with a papyrus scroll across his knees. The sculptor has made him plump, which was a sign of success and wisdom.

Write your name in hieroglyphs

Names were very important to the ancient Egyptians, who thought they were a living part of every person. A king had five names, and the last was his birth name (like your first name). Seals were used to mark papyri by pressing a carved piece of stone into soft clay.

Seals were often made in the shape of the sacred scarab beetle. Inscribed scarabs like this one were also put in coffins to protect the dead.

Use this hieroglyphic alphabet to write your name. Draw a hieroglyph of a man or woman after your name. Words were usually written from right to left and top to bottom, but could be the other way. Animal and people signs look towards the beginning of a word and tell you from which side you start to read.

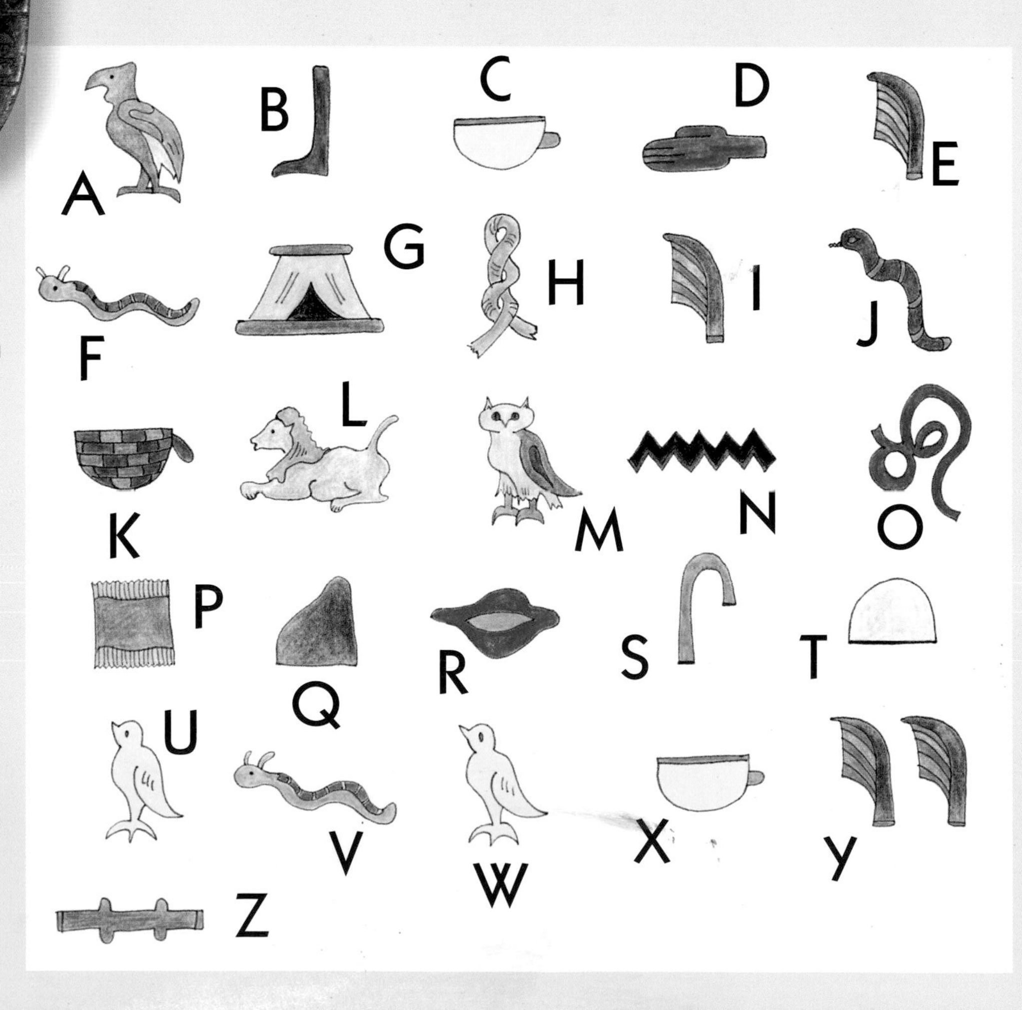

Make a scarab seal

You will need: air-hardening clay • a toothpick • a rolling pin • a modelling tool • green and blue acrylic paint • poster paint • a rolling pin • tiny beads • 2 lengths of 1-cm thick wood.

1 Mould the beetle's body and head from a lump of clay. Keep the bottom flat. Press tiny beads into the head for eyes. Mark the body and wings with a modelling tool.

2 Put two pieces of wood at the sides of a slab of clay. Roll it out until the rolling pin runs along the top of the wood.

3 Cut out an oval larger than the beetle and press the bases together. Smooth over the joint with your finger.

4 Roll a strip of clay 5mm thick. Cut out the letters of your name or initials in hieroglyphs. Leave them to harden (15 minutes). Then score the surfaces to be joined with a toothpick, moisten them and press the shapes on to the base. Make sure you put the hieroglyphs on back to front, so they print the right way round.

5 Allow the clay to dry completely, then paint the beetle green and the top of the base blue, but don't paint the hieroglyphs at the bottom.

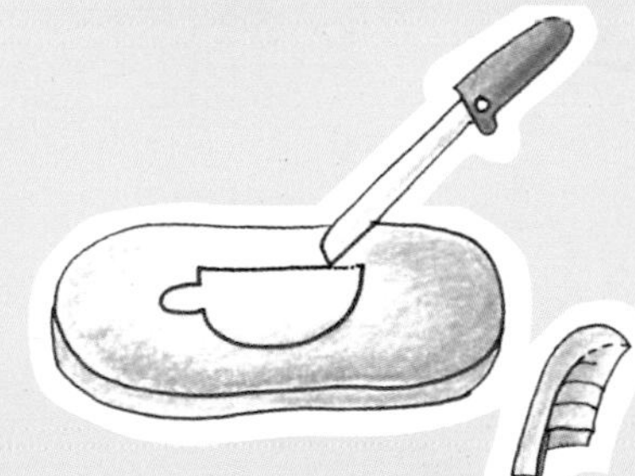

6 To print, brush a thick layer of paint over the hieroglyphs and press the scarab seal on to the paper. Wipe the clay with a wet rag before printing again.

Glossary

AD (short for Anno Domini, or 'in the year of the Lord'). This shows that a date is after the birth of Christ; AD 100 means 100 years after the birth of Christ.

archaeologist Someone who studies the ancient past by digging up and looking at remains.

BC (short for Before Christ). This shows that a date is before the Christian era (which is called AD); 100 BC means 100 years before the birth of Christ.

bellows A device that blows out a stream of air when it is squeezed.

binder A substance added to others to form a solid mass.

canopic jar A container for holding a mummified person's internal organs.

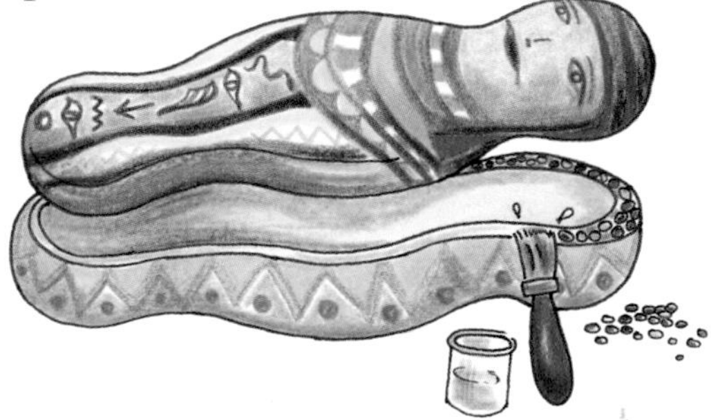

cartonnage A material made from tightly fitting layers of linen or papyrus glued together.

deity A god or goddess.

delta A fan-shaped area at the mouth of some rivers, where the river splits into many smaller channels.

draughtsman A person who makes detailed drawings.

dynasty A series of rulers from the same family.

electrum A natural mixture of gold and silver.

faience A glazed, glassy kind of pottery.

galena A black or grey mineral.

henna Red dye made from the leaves of the henna plant.

hieroglyph A symbol used in the writing system of hieroglyphics.

hieroglyphics The writing system of ancient Egypt, based on pictures and symbols representing objects and sounds.

incense A fragrant gum.

iron oxide A substance that forms rust.

kiln An oven used for firing, or baking, clay pots.

lime A white substance that comes from limestone.

manganese A dark grey metal.

master craftsman A very skilled and experienced craftsman who supervises the work of others.

mummy The body of a person or animal that has been specially prepared and preserved.

natron A mineral similar to salt, found in dry lake beds.

ochre An earthy, rusty substance that can be used to make a red colour.

palette A stone slab.

papyrus A reed plant that grows beside the River Nile, from which baskets and writing material were made.

pharaoh An ancient Egyptian ruler.

pigment The natural colour of plants or other substances that can be made into powder and used in painting.

potsherd A broken fragment of pottery.

relief A sculpture in which figures or designs stand out from the background.

sanctuary The most sacred part of a temple.

scribe A person who writes out documents.

sedge A marsh plant similar to grass.

sphinx A mythical creature with a lion's body and the head of a man, ram or bird.

stela An upright stone slab with an inscription.

twine To twist and wind (strands).

vessel A hollow container, especially for holding liquids.

Index